GOING
DEEP
&
WIDE

A COMPANION GUIDE
FOR CHURCHES AND LEADERS

ANDY STANLEY

ZONDERVAN

Going Deep & Wide
Copyright © 2017 by Andy Stanley

Portions of this book were taken from materials previously published through *Outreach* magazine. Used with permission.

This title is also available as a Zondervan ebook.

Requests for information should be addressed to:
Zondervan, *3900 Sparks Dr. SE, Grand Rapids, Michigan 49546*

ISBN 978-0-310-53830-1

Cover design: Ron Huizinga
Interior design: Kait Lamphere

Printed in the United States of America

17 18 19 20 21 22 23 24 25 /DCI/ 15 14 13 12 11 10 9 8 7 6 5 4 3 2 1

CONTENTS

Time to Rethink

Your church's mission, whether expressed in writing or not, is probably not much different from ours at North Point:

To lead people into a growing relationship with Jesus Christ
by creating irresistible churches
where people are encouraged and equipped
to pursue intimacy with God,
community with insiders,
and influence with outsiders

I'm guessing those same aims are equally meaningful to you and pretty close to your heart.

Since writing *Deep and Wide*, I've heard from pastors all over the country who are rethinking how they do church. One of the questions I'm often asked is: How do you become a church that not only helps its members pursue an intimate relationship with God but is also irresistible to those outside the church?

If your church is better at the first than the second, you're far from alone. Most churches naturally drift to serving the needs of their insiders. The gravitational pull is toward going *deep*, not wide—to focus on discipleship programs and spiritual growth for *current* church members. The people who are always there and who constantly express their needs and wants. You know: "The squeaky wheel gets the grease."

But that needs to be balanced by leadership that emphasizes how to go wide. We want our churches to be places unchurched people love to attend, places that are welcoming, engaging, helping—*irresistible*. Which brings us face-to-face with a challenge: how to develop in ourselves and in our churches an intentional awareness of outsiders.

In *Deep and Wide*, I share in detail North Point's model for going deep. As a brief refresher, early on at North Point, we agreed we were way more inspired by the people who have the kind of faith that endures a *no* from God than those who claim their faith arm-twisted a *yes* out of him. Big faith is a sign of big maturity. We concluded that the best discipleship or spiritual formation model would be one designed around growing people's faith. Conversely, the model most of us had grown up with was designed around increasing people's *knowledge*. The models we were exposed to were primarily teaching models. We wanted to go beyond that.

But how?

After a long process, we identified five dynamics that had played a role in the spiritual formation stories we heard time and time again. It was a defining moment for our team. If these dynamics were the essential ingredients in how God grew people's faith, we decided we should build our entire ministry model around them. So that's exactly what we did. While I unpack the five dynamics in detail in *Deep and Wide* and in a small group resource called *Five Things God Uses to Grow Your Faith*, I'll list them here before we move on:

The Five Faith Catalysts:

- Practical Teaching
- Private Disciplines
- Personal Ministry
- Providential Relationships
- Pivotal Circumstances

We've developed some great resources to help churches go deeper in discipleship for their insiders (see Appendix A for a sample). You might be aware of some of them or you may have borrowed discipleship activities and programs from elsewhere or even developed your own. This companion guide is *not* about turning from any of that. In fact, I encourage you to keep thinking how to further refine those programs and activities while you move forward through this guide.

Our emphasis, however, will be on the problem most of us face: *how* to create a church where the unchurched will want to come—an irresistible church where people demonstrate irresistible love and faith.

What does that kind of church look like? I spent Section Four of *Deep and Wide* on what it means to be a wide church. That content is a primer for what we'll be exploring here. But our focus on this journey is a question we started asking ourselves at North Point: *How do we know?* How do we know we're really reaching those we hope to reach? What practical things must we consider in order to gauge how well we're connecting with unbelievers? And yes, I'll share what we learned in that process.

This guide's structure is simple. First we'll dig deeper into the *why*. Why even do this? Why upset the status quo by trying to become a church where the *un*churched feel welcome? *That's bound to shake things up around here; is it worth it?* We will discover that it's worth *everything*.

In session two, we'll flesh out a sharper understanding of exactly who those unchurched people in your community are. I'll also introduce you to something I call the "Irresist List": three questions we all need to carefully think about in order to gauge our appeal to the unchurched.

The final three sessions will then zoom in on each of the Irresist List questions. We'll break each one down in detail to discover how to make our churches more attractive to outsiders.

All five sessions will include "Your Turn" sections to help your church's leadership team dive in and think hard about understanding and applying what you're reading. Let's start with one of those right now.

YOUR TURN

1. Look again at the mission statement at the start of this introduction. How closely does it reflect *your* church's mission? How strongly do you personally support your church's mission?

2. In your church, how would you compare the emphasis on going *deep* (discipleship and growth for church members) with the emphasis on going *wide* (influencing and winning outsiders)? Is greater balance needed?

3. How would you express what you want your church to become for the *un*churched people in your community? Try to capture it in a single sentence.

WHAT'S THE FAITH OF A GENERATION WORTH?

It's no secret the religious landscape in America has drastically shifted. Fewer and fewer Americans call themselves Christians, while more and more identify as religiously unaffiliated. You've heard by now how this group has been nicknamed the "nones" since they check "none of the above" on religious affiliation surveys.

A quarter of Americans are now in that group—a seven-point jump in just seven years—according to Pew Research Center's 2014 Religious Landscape Study. It's young Americans especially who fall into this category. Millennials (those born in the early 1980s through the early 2000s) make up 44 percent of the nones.

In record numbers, millennial nones are walking away from the faith they may have grown up with, the faith of their parents.[1] Surveys, podcasts, and blogs give the distinct impression that the version of faith this generation knew in childhood has left them unprepared for the rigors and questions of academia and adulthood. They exit church because they're finding the version of Christianity they were raised with is unconvincing, uninspiring, and irrelevant.

However, it's not that they perceive their understanding of Christianity as a "version" of anything, nor do they recognize that other versions out there are worth exploring. For them, their version's the *only* version. What they were raised on *is* Christianity—and it doesn't square with undeniable realities, both scientific and sociological, of the world in which they find themselves.

If we're going to reach the unchurched, underchurched, dechurched, and postchurched with the gospel in a culture that's trending post-Christian, we must rethink our approach. Changing times call for changing methods in order to accomplish our unchanging mission of making disciples.

But first, another word or two about those who are slipping out the back door.

POST-CHRISTIAN CULTURE

According to that Religious Landscape Study I mentioned, nones represent nearly 23 percent of Americans. That's just under 56 million people.

Think about that. Chances are, you're related to a none or two. You certainly know some. You've baptized some. You probably drove a few to camp. You gave them their first Bibles. You know their parents—their heartbroken, disappointed, frightened parents.

For decades we've been told we live in a postmodern culture. While we struggle to define that term, few would disagree that our culture is fundamentally different from what it used to be. If we're honest, even fewer of us in church leadership could say we've successfully adjusted our ministry approach to compensate for this radical change in reality.

Here's something else to get our heads around: We're now a *post-Christian* culture. While postmodernism rejected any idea that there's a "right" way to think and behave,[2] the post-Christian wave takes this to a frightening new level.

Here's a helpful definition from someone who's observed our culture closely:

> A post-Christian society is not merely a society where agnosticism or atheism is the prevailing fundamental belief. It's a society rooted in the history, culture, and practices of Christianity, but in which the religious beliefs of Christianity have been rejected—or worse, forgotten.[3]

There's an important distinction between *non*-Christian and *post*-Christian. The reason our evangelistic endeavors result in more recycling than actual conversion is that our methods and approaches assume non-Christian rather than post-Christian.

That must change.

In a non-Christian society, people may have never heard *anything* about Christianity; they, therefore, have few (if any) preconceived notions about it. In a post-Christian society, people *have* been exposed to Christianity (in our case, for generations) but are opting for a different worldview, a different narrative through which to make sense of the world. In a post-Christian society, people know the stories; they just don't believe them—not anymore.

The Barna Group has developed a metric for identifying a post-Christian. This metric is based on stated beliefs and practices, such as belief or disbelief in God, church attendance, spiritual practices, etc. As it turns out, more and more Americans who identify as Christians qualify as post-Christians based on their actual behavior. According to the Barna Group, 48 percent of Americans qualify as post-Christian.[4] That's nearly half of us!

Bottom line: Many—perhaps most—of the nones in America have had some connection to Christianity in their pasts, but they've rejected it. They're not non-Christian in the way we're accustomed to thinking about non-Christians. They're post-Christian, something dramatically different. This group has been there, done that, and has a closetful of camp T-shirts to show for it.

This presents a unique challenge for us in terms of apologetics and evangelism. It requires a new approach.

RESISTING THE BIBLE

For post-Christians, the go-tos for forming their worldviews are common sense, science, philosophy, and reason. Post-Christian nones have a low tolerance for faith-based answers to fact-based questions.

At the same time, they (like most Americans) aren't exactly on a truth quest. They're on a happiness quest. Many walked away from faith because faith didn't make them happy. That's not how anyone expresses it; who wants to appear that shallow? But scratch beneath the surface and you'll find the quest for happiness plays a big role. When faith is viewed as an impediment to happiness, then goodbye faith. The seemingly irrational, antiscience version of faith that many were brought up on makes it that much easier to simply walk away.

Given all that, this next statistic shouldn't come as any surprise. When asked about their views of Scripture, 72 percent of nones said it's not the Word of God.

This finding is corroborated by data compiled in a massive

study conducted from 2011 to 2016 by the Barna Group in collaboration with the American Bible Society. The study collected, tracked, and analyzed Americans' perceptions of and engagement with the Bible. The results were released in the book *The Bible in America: The Changing Landscape of Bible Perceptions and Engagement.*[5]

In the book's introduction, Barna Group president David Kinnaman outlines the study's most significant trends. Heading the list is "increased skepticism." Here's what Kinnaman says about that (if you want to stir up your next staff or elders' meeting, just pass out copies of the following excerpt):

> More people have more questions about the origins, relevance, and authority of the Scriptures. . . . The steady rise of skepticism is creating a cultural atmosphere that is becoming unfriendly—sometimes even hostile—to claims of faith. In a society that venerates science and rationalism, it is an increasingly hard pill to swallow that an eclectic assortment of ancient stories, poems, sermons, prophecies and letters, written and compiled over the course of 3,000 years, is somehow the sacred "Word of God." Even in just the few years Barna has been conducting "State of the Bible" interviews, the data is trending toward Bible skepticism. With each passing year, the percentage of Americans who believe that the Bible is "just another book written by men" increases. So does the perception that the Bible is actually harmful and that people who live by its principles are religious extremists.[6]

In 2011, 10 percent of Americans qualified as skeptics when it came to the Bible. In 2016, just five years later, that number had more than doubled. Currently, 22 percent of Americans do not believe the Bible has any divine underpinnings.[7]

But that percentage isn't the real story. The real story is the current rate at which culture is dismissing the Bible as uninspired, untrue, and irrelevant. And it doesn't stop there. Twenty-seven percent of millennial non-Christians believe "the Bible is a dangerous book of religious dogma used for centuries to oppress people."[8] Journalists, scientists, and scholars—the likes of Sam Harris, Richard Dawkins, and the late Christopher Hitchens—have provided plenty of one-sided commentary to support that narrative. Download and read Sam Harris's *Letter to a Christian Nation*, and ask yourself how well the faith of a twentysomething college student with a Sunday-school background would stand up under that kind of barrage.

Trying to appeal to post-Christian people on the basis of the authority of Scripture will have essentially the same effect as a Muslim imam appealing to you on the basis of the Quran's authority. Whether you know what the Quran says doesn't matter; it carries no weight with you. You don't view it as authoritative.

That's exactly how close to half our population views the Bible.

WHAT NOW?

As bleak as all this sounds, I'm not discouraged.

For one reason, as we all know, the original version of

our faith was extraordinarily robust. Once upon a time our faith was stronger than Roman steel and tougher than Roman nails. Against all odds, a small band of Jesus followers defied an empire and claimed that their leader came to replace the temple. Two thousand years later, we're still standing—all over the world. And we have the internet! So I'm not worried.

But I'm not sitting around praying for revival either. I grew up in the "pray for revival" culture. It's a cover for a church's unwillingness to make changes conducive to *real* revival. You want revival? *Start assuming there are post-Christian people in the room.* All your rooms. Begin evaluating through the eyes and ears of post-Christians.

Don't know any?

That may be part of the problem.

If they've come near, they've been turned off whenever you said, "the Bible says," "the Bible teaches," "God's Word is clear," or anything along those lines.

If that's the approach to preaching and teaching you grew up with—the approach you're most comfortable with and want to stick with—you're probably having a throw-down debate with me right now in your head (a debate you're winning). But before you chapter-and-verse me against the wall and put me in a sovereignty-of-God headlock, stop and ask yourself: *Why does what Andy's saying bother me so much? Why—really?*

Shifting the conversation away from the authority of Scripture to the authority, courage, and faithfulness of the men and women behind our Scriptures has not only enabled me to better connect with post-Christians, it's done wonders for the faith of the faithful. The stories of the men and women behind the Scriptures are rich and inspiring, though, unfortunately, not as well known as you might think.

For a recent example, go to WhoNeedsGod.com and watch the last ten minutes of part six. To wrap up this series, I leveraged the story of James to encourage nones to reconsider the claims of Christ, just as James the Just had to do after the resurrection of his brother. As you'll see, this in no way undermines the authority of the Bible. It actually underscores the historical roots of our Bible.

You'd be shocked by how many students and adults in our churches view the Bible as a spiritual guidebook offering true things to live by, as opposed to an inspired collection of documents reporting events that actually happened. This is why I'll continue to insist that the foundation of our faith is *not* an inspired book but the events that inspired the book—events and related conversations and insights that were documented by inspired writers borne along by the Holy Spirit. And *the* pivotal event attested to by these writers is the resurrection of Jesus.

While it's true we wouldn't know any of these events had occurred if they'd never been documented, two other things are equally true.

First, these events were documented years before there even was a "Bible," that is, a New Testament bound together with the Jewish Scriptures into a single volume.

Second, it's the *events* themselves—not the record of them—that birthed the church. The Bible did not create Christianity; Christianity is the reason the Bible was created.

Many Christians struggle with statements like these because they grew up on "the Bible says" preaching, which is fine as long as you already believe that the Bible is inspired and authoritative.

Let me state it another way. If someone is *already* convinced that the Bible is God's Word, then you can leverage "the Bible says" language. But let's be honest. What do you call people who accept the Bible as God's Word before they really understand what's in it? What do you call someone who simply takes other people's words as fact, particularly regarding something as significant as this book being God's infallible Word? What kind of person would go for that?

A child.

When did you come to believe the Bible was God's Word? Be honest. Chances are, you arrived at that conclusion the same way I did. Your momma told you. Or your pastor told you. You accepted the Bible's authority long before you read it (in my case, before I was even able to read!). Only a child would accept the Bible as God's infallible Word before knowing what was inside it.

Anything wrong with that?

I hope not. I did the same thing for my children (Richard Dawkins would say I did it *to* my children). And I'm glad I did. But this explains in part why we have a difficult time doing effective evangelism outside the circle of the already indoctrinated and the already convinced. If you're someone who didn't embrace the Bible as God's Word until adulthood, you're one of the few church leaders in that category. And those few were probably predisposed to hold the Bible in high regard as a result of some experience in childhood.

My point? If we're going to reach post-Christians, we must change the way we *talk* about the Bible. Remember, we don't live in a non-Christian culture but a post-Christian culture. Most educated people have an educated opinion about what the Bible is and isn't. They don't walk into your church with blank slates. They walk in with full slates.

That means we have to begin the conversation on the ladder's lowest rung, which isn't hard to do. And no, it doesn't require that we water things down and ignore mature believers in the room. People who think it's either/or just haven't seen it done well.

WHAT'S IT WORTH?

In a culture where the young are growing resistant to the Bible at an accelerating rate, what does that mean for the next generation and their potential for faith? And what will we do about it?

What's the faith of the next generation worth to us?

Think about that. What's the faith of your children worth? Your grandchildren?

What's it worth? I say it's worth *any change necessary* to ensure that the version of faith the next generation leaves home with is an enduring version—the faith of our first-century fathers. A version that is harder than steel and tougher than nails. A version rooted in an *event*, not a book.

So will you consider retooling your church in order to win some and save some? Are you willing to take a long, hard look—through post-Christian eyes—at everything you're currently doing? Are you ready to be a student rather than a critic?

The most counterproductive thing we can do is criticize

and refuse to learn from one another. We don't have time for petty disagreements that only those inside our own social media circles understand or care about. We don't have time for retreating into tribalism. We don't have time because *we're losing ground* in our culture at large.

We need churches that go deep *and* wide. We need this in light of what's at stake . . . and *who's* at stake.

Your Turn

1. Are the statistics and trends mentioned in this session troubling? Why do they affect you that way?

2. In light of our topic, take a few moments to read the following familiar passages. How do they inspire you to greater sensitivity, wisdom, and compassion in reaching out to those who are spiritually lost?

Matthew 9:35–38

Mark 2:15–17 and 10:42–45

Luke 15:1–10

John 3:16–17

1 Timothy 2:3–6

2 Peter 3:9

Jude 20–23

3. Review the following teachings of Jesus. What specific calling and responsibility does Jesus place on the church and the church's leadership? What might this require in the way of new attitudes and behaviors?

Matthew 5:13–16

Mark 9:50

Luke 14:34–35

John 13:34–35

4. How would you assess your own personal openness and willingness to better understand the mindset, moral values, and feelings of unchurched people in your community? What resistance or barriers to this (if

any) do you detect? What potential misconceptions or insensitivities might you have to personally face?

5. As far as you can tell, to whom do unchurched people typically look as their most trusted authorities? What are the strongest influences on their moral values and ethical standards? What holds them back from exploring faith? What evidence for this have you detected in conversations you've had with them?

6. Among the unchurched in your community, what's the typical attitude you're sensing toward Jesus as a historical person?

7. How would you answer the question asked by this session's title: "What's the Faith of a Generation Worth?"

8. How would you summarize the need you sense *in your church* for a wiser, more intentional approach to reaching the unchurched people of your community?

9. How would you assess your personal openness for pursuing any necessary changes to make your church more attractive to unchurched individuals?

THE IRRESIST
LIST AND YOUR
AUDIENCE

If we're going to do whatever it takes to help the next generation find an enduring faith—to ensure there's a church for them that's relevant and irresistible—then we'll have to look long and hard at our current methods. We'll have to stay alert for what needs to change in how we do what we do. We'll have to search for where the obstacles are and decide how to clear those away, so we become a church unchurched people love to attend.

This means we'll have the same opinion James had in Acts 15:19, where he said: "It is my judgment . . . that we should not make it difficult for the Gentiles who are turning to God." We decide that we're *not* going to make it hard for the unchurched to be with us. Every barrier, every distraction, every turnoff is something we'll seek to push aside so it's easy for unchurched men and women to attend our churches and enjoy being there.

We want them to love what they experience in our churches. And we want them to love *us*. Before they ever believe—or even if they never believe—we want to love them as God does, and we want them to sense something lovable and irresistible in who we are and what we do.

How does a church do that? How do you measure if you are winning?

As I mentioned earlier, at North Point we asked ourselves those very questions and came up with what we called the Irresist List—three questions, each with three subquestions:

1. **What do unchurched people *see*?**
   —Do our facilities look like we're expecting guests?
   —Is our brand inviting?
   —Can our guests see themselves being a part of us?
2. **What do unchurched people *hear*?**
   —What's our reputation in the community?
   —Is our communication engaging?
   —Is our content helpful?
3. **What do unchurched people *experience*?**
   —Is our communication genuine?
   —Do we respect their values and views?
   —Is our communication direct, timely, and personal?

These questions help you "go wide"—to link more broadly and effectively with the unchurched in your community. In the final three sessions of this guide, we'll explore them in depth. But before we do, I want to explore a mandate that always needs to be in front of us. It's easy to remember.

Assume They're in the Room

To make our churches irresistible for the unchurched, the first thing we have to do is assume they're in the room.

Whether it's a ministry event for college students or high schoolers or middle schoolers or a special class on marriage or a Sunday morning worship service—*assume they're in the room*.

And by "they" I mean the *unchurched*. And yes, I know you're thinking that if "they" are here in church, why keep calling them *un*churched? But trust me, at this point it's good for your sensitivity to think of them that way.

Assume they're in the room. This is a revolutionary thought for many pastors and church leaders. We sometimes forget that unchurched people are present, which means we become oblivious to things we do or say that are obstacles to the unchurched hearing what we'd like them to hear. Without even realizing it, we're making everything that much harder for them.

We drift into a mindset that our Sunday morning gatherings are safe places *just for Christians*. And as for all those *other* people—well, they're *out there* somewhere, out in the world, but definitely not in here with us.

Which is a terrible, terrible idea.

That's why these three questions on the Irresist List are so important. They continually remind us to assume those people are right here among us.

It's so easy to forget the unchurched, to be blind to them, because most church leaders aren't interacting with people outside their churches or congregations on a regular basis. By default, we craft our messages and cater our ministries to match the needs of the people who are already a part of our churches.

So how do you intentionally focus attention on the needs of people who aren't attending your church so they'll love to attend?

At North Point, my friend Jonathan Merritt has led several of our ministry areas through a simple exercise to help us define and personalize the unchurched in our community. But don't let its simplicity hide how helpful it can be. Learning to think about specific individuals who represent the unchurched man and woman you're seeking to reach will go a long way toward getting the most out of those Irresist List questions we'll cover in the next three sessions.

DEFINE YOUR "AUDIENCE"

When you're communicating, the first thing to ask is the *who* question, not the *what* question. *Who's my audience?*

Every message and ministry should have a specific audience in mind—the people you want to reach with your message and serve with your ministry, the people whose lives will be changed when you do what you do.

That's why "everyone" is never a helpful way to think of your audience. It's too broad. If you try to reach everyone, you're far more likely to fail in reaching anyone.

Asking the *who* question—and answering it thoroughly— helps you get intentional about reaching your true audience. Never set a false expectation that your content is going to reach someone it wasn't intended for.

So how do you define your true audience?

One particularly helpful way of doing this is to create a "persona"—a description of someone in particular who represents the unchurched people you wish to reach.

It's good to have a single primary persona in mind, but it's also helpful to create a primary and secondary persona to represent different elements of your audience.

Here are the steps for creating each persona:

First, define your demographic. Are you trying to reach the young urban culture, families from the suburbs, a particular ethnic group? Which specific ages are you targeting? Is there a particular education level you have in mind? A certain political bent or religious background?

You may have several demographic characteristics in mind, but try to narrow down the list so it more closely matches the unchurched person you're seeking to reach in your community.

Second, sketch a "psychographic" profile. While demographic data speaks to outward characteristics such as age, gender, and geography, a psychographic analysis looks at felt needs and inner desires. This helps you get in touch with people's ways of thinking and their emotions. Ask questions like these: *What does our audience want most in life? What are they afraid of? What wakes them up in the morning and gets them going? What keeps them awake in the middle of the night? What makes them cry? What makes them give of themselves?* You want to have a good picture of their core struggles—the emotions and needs they're struggling with or seeking to have met.

Third, name them. Make this personal. Give each persona you create a name. Don't worry about labels—the goal of this is to care for real people, to help you better connect with the unchurched in your community. A name for the persona you create helps you keep the unchurched in mind in a concrete way.

Fourth, continue refining this persona. Learn and adjust. As you navigate the next three sessions, you may want to change some elements of the personas you develop. No problem. Plan to refine each persona over time as you use it to create content and cater your ministry approach to better meet the needs of unchurched people.

PERSONA: AN EXAMPLE

Here's an example of a primary persona we created for one of our ministries:

Name: Dissatisfied Drew
Age: 32
Marital status: Single
Kids: None
Education: Four-year degree
Financial status: Comfortable, has 401(k), credit card debt, leases an Audi
Health: Has gym membership (rarely uses), softball league, bad diet, overindulges
Spiritual development: Formal religious exposure, been through season of indifference (becoming dissatisfied), listens to audiobooks on leadership to grow and find purpose
Attitude toward church: Cynical about organized religion, a "none," wouldn't overthink a casual invite to church
Core struggles: (1) boredom; (2) regret; (3) loneliness; (4) anxiety; (5) laziness; (6) low-grade anger; (7)

dissatisfaction; (8) lack of purpose; and (9) blaming others rather than taking ownership

Core needs: (1) direction in life; (2) freedom from guilt/shame; (3) improved relationships; opportunities to gather with others; (4) peace and freedom from worry; (5) motivation and encouragement to be more intentional and to change; (6) peace in relationships; emotional awareness; (7) contentment with current life; (8) sense of purpose and awareness of new possibilities; and (9) taking responsibility for actions

By accurately zeroing in on these kinds of details, you'll sharpen your focus on the unchurched—making you more aware that *they're really there.*

YOUR TURN

1. As a warm-up to this session's exercise, take a few minutes to think together about typical characteristics of unchurched people in your community—just a quick list of representative traits, especially regarding their likes and dislikes, values and beliefs, habits and actions, assumptions and attitudes.

   Next, narrow your focus by imagining a primary and secondary persona of unchurched individuals and creating a detailed description for each one. You'll attach specific facts and traits to them, and eventually name each one. Try to select details that would be reasonably typical of unchurched people in your community.

In your group, you can all take part in deciding on each detail. Or—more quickly—you can take turns assigning each detail, and afterward the full group can further refine each persona.

At first we'll label each persona as "Primary" or "Secondary," until you later decide on their names.

2. Complete the following chart to assign background details for each persona:

	Primary	Secondary
Age:		
Marital Status:		
Number and Ages of Children:		
Education Level:		
Neighborhood They Live In:		
Current Employment:		
Current Financial Status:		
Vehicle(s) Owned:		
Current Health (summarize):		
Exercise Habits:		
Stress Relievers (friends, alcohol, hobbies, etc.)		
Other _____		

3. In the spiritual/religious category, answer these questions for each persona.

- How would you describe this person's previous exposure (if any) to formal religion?

   Primary:

   Secondary:

- How would you describe this person's present attitude toward church and Christianity?

   Primary:

   Secondary:

- How would you describe this person's previous exposure (if any) to the Bible?

   Primary:

Secondary:

- How would you describe this person's present attitude toward Jesus as a historical person?

  Primary:

  Secondary:

4. For each persona, answer the following questions:

- List words or phrases that describe this person's core struggles—the ways in which they sense inadequacy, anxiety, fear, or frustration—and the emotions they frequently experience as a result.

  Primary:

  Secondary:

- For each of the core struggles listed above for each persona, what do they need to experience or discover in order to best resolve that struggle?

  Primary:

  Secondary:

5. Now give a name to each persona—ideally a two-part name (descriptive adjective plus first name), such as my "Dissatisfied Drew" example.

   Primary:

   Secondary:

6. How helpful has this exercise of creating these personas been for your group? How does it help you identify ways to be more sensitive to unchurched people in your community?

7. How often have you observed guests in your church that closely match one of these personas? What can you do to be more aware of them when they visit?

8. As you interact with unchurched individuals in the future, what can help you better understand each person's core struggles and core needs? To gain this understanding, what will be required of you?

session three

WHAT DO
UNCHURCHED
PEOPLE *SEE?*

Now back to the Irresist List—the three questions we need to ask for "going wide" to create a church unchurched people love to attend. In this session, let's drill in on the first question: *What do unchurched people see when they attend our church?*

To answer that, consider three vital ingredients:

- Is our "brand" inviting?
- Do our church facilities give the impression we're expecting guests to arrive?
- Can unchurched people see themselves in our church? Does it look like the kind of place they could belong?

IS OUR BRAND INVITING?

The first ingredient to consider is our brand identity. Is it inviting? Is it attractive?

When I talk about branding, I'm initially talking about that part of us people see *before* they get here. This includes our social media, our church website, anything that represents us visually online as well as in the community.

The whole concept of branding may not be something you like or feel comfortable about, but it's a reality you need to deal with. When people look at your church from a distance, they may not have a personal connection to any particular person there. They won't know much about you, except for what they can see from that distance. *That* is your brand at the widest point. It's how you present yourself to those who don't know you, how they see you in their first interactions with you.

As we think about our brand, we need to ask: What does it communicate about who we are and who our church is for? Some churches communicate that they're only for Christians—the unchurched need not apply.

At the end of the day, branding is not just a logo, fonts, colors, or a "style." Those are merely things we choose to help people initially identify and then consistently recognize our brand. Ultimately, *our brand is what people believe is true about us.* The words and emotions people use to describe their experiences with us. What's "remarkable" about us— that is, worth being remarked about.

Our brand has to do with our consistency in creating a feel that makes us appealing and, above all, trustworthy. The right brand has to be lived out—genuinely and consistently— before it's real.

Ideally, at the outset of development, the branding process brings to the forefront the *why* of our existence as a church or ministry. That process begins when we ask questions like these:

- What do we want people to know immediately when they first encounter us?
- What do we hope they'll remember about their interactions with us?
- What do we want them to tell their friends about us? What do we hope they *won't* say about us?

Once we have a sense of confidence about these things and the brand is developed, the hard part begins—keeping the brand focused. Staying focused will make people comfortable because they'll know what to expect. Consistency is key. People will ultimately judge us by their full experience, not just one part. But it starts with what they see. *All* of it matters— everything we do. It's an expression of what we'll be known by.

In today's culture where people are bombarded by messaging, only those whose lives match their messages will succeed. *Who we are* has to mirror the experience we desire to create for the unchurched once they step through our doors. When that's true, then people will feel proud to invite others to our church. That's something we can't lose sight of—because the mission we're called to is far too important.

Your Turn

1. How would you describe your church's current brand? Does it communicate who you really are and who your church is for? Is it welcoming to the unchurched?

2. What, if anything, would you like to change about your church's brand?

3. What do you most want people to immediately know about you when they first encounter anything about your church?

4. What do you hope your church's guests will remember most about their experiences with you?

5. What would you like your church's guests to tell their friends about you? What do you hope they *won't* say about you?

6. When you think about the ideal brand for your church, what will be involved in truly living it out so that it's *real*?

&

Do Our Facilities Communicate That We're Expecting Guests?

The next ingredient we need to think about is our facilities. How do they look? What does their appearance communicate to outsiders? *Does it send the message that we're expecting them—and their children?* When they walk in on a Sunday morning, or when they drive into the parking lot, is everything giving the signal, "You're welcome here"?

View your facilities with fresh eyes, like you do at home when important guests are coming. When your spouse's boss or your son or daughter's future in-laws are expected at your house for dinner, think about how you go that extra mile to make sure the place is clean and organized. And once they arrive, as host you stay conscious of the fact that there are certain things you talk about with your guests and certain things you don't. You maintain graciousness and respect and tact in your conversations because, after all, they're your *guests*—in *your* home!

That should be our mindset in the church, but it's where many churches fall short.

When I visit other churches, I find myself looking at everything as an outsider, someone who doesn't regularly attend there. Sometimes what I see isn't very welcoming. It's hard to avoid the sense that nobody has walked through the place with fresh eyes in a long time. I feel like I've entered someone's home when they weren't expecting visitors. But the church's leaders probably can't see any of that because it's invisible to them.

Every environment communicates something. The physical appearance of your facility really matters, particularly as you think about the people you're trying to appeal to.

Your church's environments should be *clean*. Why? Because a clean place communicates that we're expecting you, that you matter to us, that you're our guest.

It should also be *organized*—which communicates that we're serious about what we're doing. You need to be overly, intentionally organized on the front end, especially for your weekend services and your children's ministry.

Your environment also should be *safe*, which says that we value your kids the way we value our own.

An uncomfortable or distracting physical environment—whether it's in your children's ministry area, in the hallways, or in the parking lot—can derail ministry before it ever begins. Sandra and I once visited a church for the first time and arrived a little early. There were no signs or directions anywhere, and we didn't know where to go. We finally found someone who could point us to the children's ministry area. With our toddler Andrew, we walked into a room that was empty except for a guy who looked like he was in his twenties, sitting in a chair at a table. In the back of the room was a door leading outside, with daylight shining in.

Put yourself in our position as parents, faced with whether to leave our toddler son alone with that guy in that situation. Can you imagine how uncomfortable that was? Ministry was derailed, and we hadn't even gotten to the sermon yet.

We decided to leave Andrew there, but as the first song began, Sandra turned to me and whispered, "Do you feel good about Andrew's situation?" I said no, and she was gone for the rest of the service to make sure another adult was in that classroom.

Every physical environment communicates something— and how we design and decorate our facilities communicates who we want to be.

I have a friend who leads a church in Phoenix. They built a new building, and several nice ladies wanted to be in charge of decorating the entrance foyer. He didn't think anything of it and told them to make it look nice. When he came in the first Sunday, there were flowers everywhere. It smelled good, and it was beautiful. But after a few weeks, he noticed that the only people hanging out in the foyer were a bunch of ladies. So he went down to the Harley dealership and asked if the manager would mind parking a couple of his motorcycles in the church lobby the next weekend. They did some repainting and parked the Harleys there. The following Sunday they had large groups of men hanging out there.

Evaluate everything about your facility's design and décor. Your attention to detail will communicate what and who you value most.

YOUR TURN

1. How would you describe your church facilities and the current environment associated with each of your church's various gatherings?

2. What would it take to get "fresh eyes" on each of these environments?

3. Identify your target audience for each environment. Does the existing physical setting communicate that you're expecting guests? How can each environment be improved to more strongly appeal to your target audience?

4. Do the design, décor, and attention to detail of your environments reflect what and who is most important to you?

5. Is there any aspect of these environments that is starting to look tired? If so, what kind of makeover is needed?

DO THEY SEE THEMSELVES HERE?

The last ingredient to consider is whether unchurched visitors can easily see themselves fitting in at your church. *Do they see themselves here?* Can they envision being a part of this community? Can they easily see themselves helping to serve in some capacity—greeting at the door, checking in kids, being part of the worship team, or whatever?

To get the best answers, we need to flip the questions: Who's having a *hard* time seeing themselves fitting in at our church? What are the barriers that prevent them from wanting to belong?

Then ask: How can we remove those barriers? How can we help these people feel there's a place for them here? How can we make it easier for them to get involved? How can we help them find their spots, those places where they'll say, "I've found my people; here's where I want to serve"?

This is a big deal, far bigger than most of us realize. Have you ever attended services at a church and left thinking, *Man, who would ever want to attend this church*? But you look around and realize there are hundreds of people here who look like regulars. Why do they keep coming back? More often than not, the reason is that they've found their community. There's a relational connection for them there. And when you've found your people, you'll put up with a whole lot of stuff. When you're with your people, you'll put up with mediocre food at a restaurant or mediocre music at a concert. In a community of folks you've grown comfortable with, you'll tolerate all kinds of things.

As Christians, we're called to love each other. And we want to love one another in such a way that outsiders will see it and say, "Wow, I want to be a part of that."

So keep asking: *Do they see themselves here?* I think this question, maybe more than any other, will spark creativity and innovation in your church. It's something we need to be sensitive to, because if you can see *your* people in the church, you can easily be blind to the fact that other people can't see themselves there.

You also want to ask, "Who's *not* here? Who are we missing?"

At North Point, our 9:00 a.m., 11:00 a.m., and 4:30 p.m. services are Strollerville, USA—lots of young families. While that's great, we've realized that if you are a twenty-four-year-old single, you just won't see yourself in our church at any of those services. And the big problem is, if you don't see yourself there, you're less likely to bring your friends. This was definitely happening at North Point among our twentysomethings.

I was out with our lead pastor, Clay Scroggins, at lunch one day and we started a conversation with the woman serving our table. She was twenty-four, living at home in her parents' basement, and she mentioned she'd been looking around for a church. We asked if she'd tried North Point.

She said no, she hadn't, and then added this: "I think a lot of my parents' friends attend there."

Sirens went off immediately. Afterward I told Clay, "Where would we even invite her? She'd probably get lost in our services."

That moment led us to begin thinking about how to create a service for the twentysomethings in our community. We wanted them to feel like they had a place they could see themselves attending, belonging, and serving.

That's the kind of careful thought we should give regarding every audience segment we want to reach—so that more people can truly and easily see themselves as being a part of us.

YOUR TURN

1. List the different types of people and age groups for which your church offers unique environments. Think about the opportunities each environment offers for capturing the hearts, imaginations, and attention of that audience. What is it about each environment that can either help or hinder this process?

2. How do you address the unchurched guests that may be in your audience? In what ways are they acknowledged and welcomed? Discuss the specific language that is used—how effectively does it make unchurched guests feel they belong?

3. If you were going to launch a new service targeted at a demographic that's currently underrepresented in your services, who would you choose to reach?

In what ways would this service need to be different from your church's current services?

4. Think back to the two personas you developed in session two, and review their characteristics. For each persona, what do you envision as the most important factors that make them either comfortable or uncomfortable in your church's various environments?

Primary:

Secondary:

5. For each of those personas, what exactly would they need to experience at your church so they'll start thinking, *I can really see myself becoming a part of this*?

Primary:

Secondary:

6. How can you stay more alert to the ways unchurched guests react to what they see in your church?

WHAT DO
UNCHURCHED
PEOPLE *HEAR*?

What are people hearing—*in* your church and *about* your church? That's the second question on the Irresist List.

Three ingredients can help us further unpack this question—three practical realities to consider as we think about how we communicate with the unchurched:

- What's our reputation in this community?
- Is our communication engaging to unchurched people?
- Is our content helpful to them?

What's Our Reputation?

Our reputation is simply the word of mouth that's out there about the experiences people have had with us. In other words, *what are we known for?* Do we have a good reputation in our community? Is what we're known for what we *want* to be known for?

The distinguishing mark of the early Christians was their compassion and generosity—it is what *they* were known for. In the culture of that time, reciprocation was the norm: you gave in order to get something in return. But Christians gave of themselves to others without such expectation.

Jesus had walked into that culture and announced that his kingdom would be different. He taught his disciples to give without anticipating repayment, to lend knowing they might not get their stuff back. Jesus taught his followers to love their enemies. He redefined *neighbor* to include those who were on the outside, those who were rejected, disliked, and despised by the majority. He revolutionized their understanding of leadership and influence, teaching that these were to be used to serve others, not themselves.

Sociologist Rodney Stark writes that when sickness hit a region and the population fled to escape it, the early Christians remained behind to serve the sick and diseased. As a result, many pagans left their idolatrous ways and embraced Christianity.[9] Generosity, compassion, and love were the hallmarks of the first-century church, and that proved to be more influential than any political power or monetary wealth.

The generosity and compassion of Christians changed the world once. What would happen if the church became known for such behavior again?

Let me encourage you and your church to work hard to develop a good reputation by living out the call of Jesus. Do good! Be rich in good deeds, as the apostle Paul encourages us. Be generous and willing to share with those in need in your community.

When it comes to the topic of generosity, I've been known to be uncomfortably bold. It began with a message series I preached in 2007 called *How to Be Rich*. Two things prompted the series. First, our culture's incessant messages about how to get rich when, in fact, most of us are already rich compared to the rest of the world. And second, Paul's instructions to Timothy regarding how rich Christians were to behave. After studying the passage, I was left with the realization that a lot of rich Christians are not very good at being rich. Then it dawned on me: Well, of course, they're not. Nobody has taught them how! So for four weekends, I navigated our congregation through the terms and conditions of Paul's instructions to rich people.

The next year, I followed up with a message on the same topic and a month-long generosity campaign aimed at our local community. The campaign included a hefty donation goal, and in addition to financial support for local and international charities, we asked our people to donate two or three hours of their time that month to volunteer at the charities we'd chosen to receive the funds collected.

And by the way, none of these charities had asked us for money. That's what made it all so fun.

Behind the scenes, a team of church staff and volunteers went into our local communities to identify charities already making a measurable difference but that could use a little wind in their sails. You can imagine their surprise when a handful of folks from our church showed up with big checks! This was not money they were expecting.

But the impact went beyond those charities. A few weeks later, we opened our services with a video of staff and volunteers at these charities receiving their surprise donations. Not a dry eye in the place. Suddenly and simultaneously, everybody at North Point experienced the truth of Jesus' words that it is more blessed to give than to receive.

And we have done this campaign every year since. In the fall 2016, our churches raised $5.8 million toward this generosity initiative. And we gave 100 percent of it away. No shipping and handling costs. No overhead or operating expenses. No expensive vacations for the pastor and his family. We gave it all away. In addition, our congregants provided 51,449 volunteer hours to local charities that were volunteer-dependent.

I realize you and your church are already doing amazing things in your community and around the world. I assume you have your own stories to tell. I simply want to remind you that one of the ways unchurched people will hear about your church is by your reputation in the community. And one of the best ways to develop that reputation is to live out what Jesus commands of us by being generous with your time and your finances.

On this point, Jesus could not have been clearer. It's not what you have that matters. It's what you *do* with what you have that will matter. And just so we're clear here, I'm not a philanthropist. While I care about the poor, the issue of local or global poverty doesn't keep me up at night. I'm concerned for the plight of children. But I'm not on a mission to get all the available orphans in the world adopted into Christian homes. Though, like you, I wish they could be. My passion is my concern for the reputation and cultural positioning of the local church. I want to reanchor the church to undeniable, mind-boggling, culture-shifting demonstrations of compassion and mercy. That was the hallmark of the early church. And that got people's attention.

How well are you doing this? Be honest here. When people think of your church, what comes to mind? And is that the reputation you want?

YOUR TURN

1. How would you assess your church's reputation in your community? What's your church most known for, especially among unchurched people? What particular evidence leads you to this assessment?

2. As far as you can discern, what do your unchurched guests remember about visiting your church? What are they telling their friends about your church?

3. To what degree is there overall consistency in the impressions unchurched guests have about your church?

4. In your community, how would you describe the relationship between the reputation of Jesus and the reputation of your church?

5. How much are the people in your church actively involved in generous, compassionate service toward others in your community? How rich are they in good deeds? What specifics in this regard can you mention?

IS THE COMMUNICATION ENGAGING?

You also need to consider your church's spoken communication—the songs that are sung, the verbal announcements that are made during a service, and the message that is shared. *Are they engaging?*

By *engaging*, I'm not talking about providing entertainment for people. Think *emotional*. Are we creating an emotional connection? Are we engaging people beyond a surface level, speaking to the depths of their hearts?

When people go to their doctors, they aren't looking for emotional connections. They just want information. But in most arenas of life, we want emotional connections. We crave communication that strikes an emotion or creates some connection with us at a deeper level. That's why people love attending a good movie or a great concert. These experiences don't just give us something to think about; they stir our emotions and connect in a way that goes beyond the factual.

When communication is engaging, that content gets caught up quickly in emotion.

I think most church leaders assume far too much here. We all suffer from the curse of knowledge. We know so much about what we do and how we do it. And knowing so much, it's almost impossible for us not to assume that what people really want is to interact with all that information. But that's not what they want. They far more deeply want their hearts to be stirred than for their minds to be stretched.

To really engage is to secure another's attention in a way that touches both mind *and* heart.

The church is in the presentation business. That's what we do, our primary responsibility: we present. Engaging presentations of the gospel are central to the success of our mission.

At North Point, we decided early on that at every single level of our organization, we wanted to have highly engaging communication. We said that if anybody's going to strap on a wireless mic, narrate a video, or make an announcement, it has to be engaging. It's not enough for the content to be true.

And just having a certain position doesn't qualify anyone to get up in front and say something. No, if you can't engage our audience, you don't get the microphone.

Here's why. People stop attending because they're disengaged, not because they disagree. Nine times out of ten, when people stop attending your church, it's not because they dislike something you've said (though they might) but because they were bored and disengaged.

Lots of people come to our church who disagree with us about many things. But they keep coming back because we've engaged them, we've engaged their children, we've engaged their teenagers.

Someone can get up and tell a story you already know, but you're hanging on to the edge of your seat, captivated by it. What's drawing you in? It's not the information but the presentation. Which means that if you're going to have someone open up the pages of Scripture and present God's Word, that person needs to be engaging. The truth is true, but it has to be presented in a way that's engaging. In fact, the quality of your presentation will determine the attention span of your audience.

Have you ever listened to a comedian? Comedians have no point; they have no visual aids; their content has no practical application; and they have nothing helpful to say. But forty-five minutes later, you're looking at your watch amazed that the time has passed.

If we're going to talk about the most important information in the world, we need to decide up front that we're not going to bore children with the Word of God, we're not going to put teenagers to sleep with the Word of God, and we're not going to numb the minds of their parents with the Word of God. Because the extent to which that content engages people is going to determine whether they see it as relevant to their lives.

YOUR TURN

1. What are the best ways to determine if your church's communication is truly *engaging* to your unchurched guests?

2. Is what's engaging to you the same as what's engaging to an unchurched person? If not, what's the difference? And how does that relate to making your church communication engaging?

3. What steps can you take to improve the quality of the presentations in your church? What can be done

to keep audiences engaged even when they don't agree with your content?

4. Does your system allow you to put your best presenters in your most strategic presentation environments? Are the people presenting content in your environments the most gifted at engaging and teaching their respective audiences? If not, what systems could be put in place that would allow content to be created by the best creators and presented by the best presenters? In what ways could volunteers be used to form these partnerships?

5. In your church, are the presenters of content evaluated and coached?

6. Think of this concept in light of the various ways Jesus engaged others as he taught. How was his content not only true but also engaging? How should those same communication qualities be reflected in your church's communication?

Is the Communication Helpful?

Finally, when you consider what an unchurched attendee hears at your church or in one of your services, you have to ask if the content is actually helpful.

I'm going to assume your content will be true and biblical, but is it also presented in a helpful way? What would a first-timer do with what he or she just heard in your church? What about a middle schooler or high school student?

This question—*Is the content helpful?*—applies to any environment where a presenter in your church is communicating. Is what they're sharing actually helping people?

What we've learned is that if people are resisting at the macro level, they may be thinking, *I'm not sure there's a God; I'm not sure I take the Bible seriously; I've heard some questionable things about the New Testament.* But content that's helpful in a real and practical way can break through some of that resistance and lower the barriers. People who sit skeptically through a service may pick up on just one helpful point about marriage or childrearing and leave that morning thinking, *Okay, that's something I can use.* It's a positive takeaway for them.

As I speak, I often try to pull something practical out of a message and make that explicit to an unchurched attendee. I'll say, "You don't have to be a Christian to do this. This isn't a Christian thing; this is just something good to know." That's my way of saying, "Here's something helpful for you, whether or not you buy into everything we believe and say." The content we're sharing is true, yes. And it's biblical. That's nonnegotiable. But we also want to communicate what's *helpful* about it, whether you're a Christian or not.

Again, we're not satisfied with our content simply being true. If it's coming out of the Bible, we know it's true. But that's not where we need to start with the unchurched people who are listening. They want to know if it's helpful—and when I say *helpful*, I mean *useful*.

Helpful content is directly addressed to how we live. This is part of the magic of creating an environment where unchurched people will come back week after week, even if they don't believe what you're saying. As long as they think it's helpful, they'll continue to come and listen.

In fact, I'll often give unbelievers permission *not* to believe what I'm saying, while encouraging them to try it at home anyway: "Now you may not believe this is true; you may not believe the Bible's inspired. But I'm just telling you, try this at home. Not because the Bible says it, but just try it.

It's helpful." We have Jewish people and Muslims who attend, and they will admit they don't believe in Jesus. But they come because it's helpful to them and to their lives. Should that be offensive to us? No. I'm so glad these people are coming. But I also know it's dangerous for them to come here. Because if they start hanging around with the body of Christ for very long, they may start believing some of those things Jesus taught and said.

Here's the deal. You and I can't make people fall in love with Jesus, but we can set up the dates, right? I share *helpful* things, *useful* things, because I want them to come back for the second date—and the third and the fourth. If people say, "I don't want to follow Jesus," I can't make them follow him, but I can try to convince them to come on back for another date.

For content to be helpful, it needs to be age-specific. Years ago, my friend Reggie Joiner said, "All Scripture is equally inspired, but it's not all equally applicable." And though all Scripture's inspired, not all of it is appropriate for every age. And before you accuse me of saying parts of the Bible don't apply, I believe this is exactly what the New Testament models for us.

The New Testament epistles illustrate how Paul wrote directly to specific issues being experienced by specific churches in specific places. He observed the problem and said, "You've got this issue; here's what you need to do about that." Paul bounced all over the place, because he was talking to real people about real things. He drew from the broader Word of God, from the story line of the entire Bible, and applied that to the specific issues the church faced.

Why don't we do what Paul did? We should. It's what makes content helpful.

Years ago, North Point staff sat down and asked, "What does a teenager need to know? What does a middle schooler need to know?" We wanted to provide them with the most helpful content that's appropriate for their age—the questions they're asking and the issues they're wrestling with.

Information that doesn't address a felt need is perceived as irrelevant. It may not actually be irrelevant, but it's *perceived* as irrelevant. When you present information without communicating that it's going to answer a question they've been asking or address something they've been feeling or solve a mystery they want solved—if you don't set it up for them and show them why it matters to them—it will likely be perceived as irrelevant. And irrelevance just doesn't stick.

Even the most skeptical people in the world want to know how to deal with their fear, their pain, their anger, with those who treat them poorly. We share so many felt needs with the fellow members of our community that it should be easy for us to bring to bear remedies from God's Word. Then, even if they don't believe Jesus is the Messiah, even if they don't believe he's their Savior, they can walk away saying, "I don't know that I believe everything they believe, but that was so helpful."

This has nothing to do with creating new ideas or changing the stories of the Bible. It has everything to do with how you present what you've been teaching in a way that's helpful.

YOUR TURN

1. Keeping in mind the difference between "true" and "helpful," to what extent is the content delivered in your environments helpful? Share some examples of content that even an unbeliever would find relevant and could use to enhance his or her thinking and living. Are you regularly providing a "takeaway" for the unchurched person who attends?

2. To what extent do your content creators and communicators understand that the goal of content communication is application and changed behaviors?

3. What audience do you have in mind as you develop your content? In addition to thinking of someone of a certain age and in a specific stage of life, are you thinking about someone who's unchurched? What is

that person looking for? What felt needs is he or she seeking to have addressed?

4. Think again about each of the personas you developed in session two. For each of them, what examples can you give of message content that would be particularly helpful on a practical level in their lives?

Primary:

Secondary:

5. As we observe Jesus in the Gospels, in what ways was his spoken content not only true but also helpful? And how can those principles be applied to content presented in your church?

6. Review the principles Paul expresses in 1 Corinthians 9:19–23. How does this passage most relate to the issues of your church's engaging communication and helpful content for unchurched guests?

WHAT DO
UNCHURCHED
PEOPLE *EXPERIENCE?*

And now the final question on our Irresist List: *What do unchurched people experience?* What do your unchurched guests experience when they come to your church? Is it something positive? Did they enjoy themselves? Did the time go by fast? Is this something they'll consider getting out of bed for and doing again?

After a service, I may ask myself: "Was what happened here worth it?" Because that's the question all those people leaving our crowded parking lots are asking themselves. *Was what I just did worth it?* If you have two kids, and they exit our children's classrooms happy, saying how much they want to come back, then as a parent you're thinking, *That was worth it. They got something out of this, and so did I.*

As you evaluate the experience unchurched people have in your church, here are important ingredients to consider:

- Are we genuine?
- Are we showing respect for the views and values of our unchurched guests?
- When we respond to their stated questions or concerns, is our communication direct, timely, and personal?

ARE WE GENUINE?

The unchurched people among you may well be thinking, *They don't believe what I believe, and I don't believe what they believe.* But will they also get the impression that we *genuinely* believe what we believe, and that we're genuine people?

Another way to think about this is to ask ourselves if we're *approachable.* Will our guests think the people on the stage seemed approachable and real? Or did it feel like a show, like a production disconnected from real life? Did the pastor feel approachable in what he said and how he communicated it? The woman who checked in my kids—did she seem like a robot? Or like a real person with her own real kids, someone who obviously knows what it's like to be a parent?

Bridging the genuineness gap and the approachability gap between the person on the platform and the person in the audience is a big deal. Because you can get everything right on the platform and still not come across as genuine or authentic or approachable. You may give yourself an "A" for a great sermon or a high-five for the great music and singing. Everything may have been perfectly executed. But if it's perfectly executed and it doesn't bridge the gap from the stage to the people who've attended, then you've failed.

I heard John Maxwell say years ago that people have to buy into the communicator before they'll buy into the communication. They're asking themselves: *Do I trust this person, or is he trying to sell me something? Do I trust that lady up there, or is she just going through her little shtick? Sure, she had some funny lines, and she got through the announcements with flying colors. But is she for real? Or is she a paid actress? Does she even attend this church?*

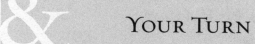

YOUR TURN

1. What do you consider the most important factors in helping unchurched people sense the genuineness, approachableness, and trustworthiness of those they interact with and hear from in your church?

2. In what important ways do the following passages assist church leaders (and all Christians) in their commitment to genuineness, approachability, and trustworthiness?

   Romans 12:3–8

   1 Corinthians 2:1–5

   2 Corinthians 2:17

   James 3:13

ARE WE SHOWING RESPECT FOR THEIR VIEWS AND VALUES?

A second ingredient to help us gauge people's experience is to ask the question: *Do we show respect for their views and values?*

I think this is where many churches really mess up. We forget that unchurched people have worldviews that are legitimate and very meaningful to them, however different from our own. And they didn't get to their worldviews because they rejected ours. They got to their worldviews the same way all of us do—because it's how we were raised. It's what we've been taught, the product of what we've experienced. It's a bad idea to reject categorically—or even accidentally—someone else's worldview. It's also foolish, because you're burning your bridges. Once you've rejected something that's so deeply and personally a part of them, it doesn't really matter what else you say or how nicely you say it. They're already done with you.

If I feel like you've rejected my worldview before you've really gotten to know me—before you've heard my story—you cannot influence me. You can be right, but you'll never influence me.

This is glaringly true on social media. Christians who interact with the unchurched on social media need to exercise wisdom and show grace. Those qualities are needed online just as much as they're needed when you interact with someone face-to-face. We should constantly be asking, "Am I showing respect for this person's views and values?"

Be sure to communicate, "I can understand why you hold that view. I can understand why that's something you value so highly. I totally get that. I totally accept that you have good reasons for holding those views and values." Communicate respect for their beliefs as well as for the reasons behind those beliefs. Because everything people believe makes sense to them even if it seems crazy to us. If we don't understand why people hold a specific value or particular belief, the problem isn't with them, but with us. We need to listen and seek to understand before we assume that we know.

Until we can argue their case in a way that seems right to them, we may just need to shut up. Which is why I try to validate other worldviews and other perspectives as often as possible. Because in the minds and hearts of unchurched people, these beliefs are totally valid. It's the loving thing to do . . . and also the right thing to do, if from only a practical perspective. Because when people sense that we genuinely respect their views and values, the door starts easing open for us to influence them.

One more thing on this—something important: avoid poking fun at other people's worldviews. Several years ago, in a continuing ministry we sponsored, we invited a guest pastor from California to speak on sex and dating. He was good at this, but he forgot the mandate I mentioned earlier—*assume they're in the room.* During his talk, he took a shot at Britney Spears. What he didn't know was that only two months earlier, Britney Spears had actually attended that very service. She'd slipped in with her bodyguards and listened to the message.

After this pastor finished his talk, I confronted him and told him what I just told you. And I said, "I'm so glad she wasn't here tonight to hear your joke at her expense. But here's what I want you to learn from this. You need to teach as if she's here every night. You need to teach as if the person you're about to make fun of is in this room."

If we follow the mandate—if we assume they're in the room—it helps create instant respect for their views and values.

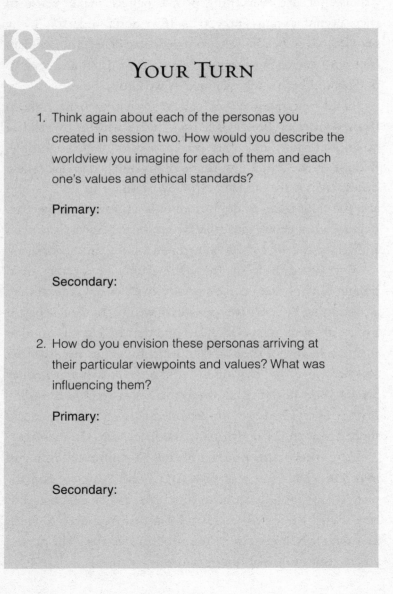

YOUR TURN

1. Think again about each of the personas you created in session two. How would you describe the worldview you imagine for each of them and each one's values and ethical standards?

   Primary:

   Secondary:

2. How do you envision these personas arriving at their particular viewpoints and values? What was influencing them?

   Primary:

   Secondary:

3. How deeply and sympathetically do you think you can understand the way an unchurched person arrives at his or her values and viewpoints? What might hinder you from such understanding?

4. On a personal level, what could you do practically and lovingly to show more respect for this person's views and values (without compromising your own)?

Primary:

Secondary:

5. Look again at the principles Paul states in 1 Corinthians 9:19–23, which you also examined in session four. How does this passage relate to the issue of respecting the views and values of others?

6. Look also at Paul's experiences in Acts 17:16–34. How did he show respect in Athens for the views and values of his listeners?

7. Why exactly is such respect necessary before true influence can occur?

8. When unchurched people visit your church, what kind of statements or actions in your services could potentially convey contempt or disrespect to them?

Do We Respond Quickly, Directly, and Personally?

Finally, when we think about our unchurched guests, we need to ask: *Do we respond quickly, directly, and personally?*

In the foyer after the service or in a phone call or in an email, an unchurched person will sometimes communicate a question, a concern, or a complaint. If we want to create a church that unchurched people love to attend, we have to respond quickly, directly, and personally.

If we respond that way when they mention something negative they've experienced with us, then in essence we're saying, "We're genuinely sorry you had a bad experience at our church. We work hard to keep that from happening. But we've failed you, and we're sorry. Is there anything we can do to make that up to you?" That's a powerful, powerful thing.

We've developed seven guiding principles to help us respond to questions from people who are new or visiting the church.

1. *Communicate we want something* for *them, not* from *them.* When unchurched people first attend your church, they may come with a sense that the church wants their money, their time, or some kind of up-front commitment. So communicate clearly that you're here to serve them.

2. *Say no as "personally" as possible.* We can't meet every need, and we won't be able to change our existing programs to accommodate every request. But when we must say no, we want to communicate in a way

that's helpful, pointing them to other resources or
ministries if possible.

3. *Make sure the person feels heard.* People feel valued
   when they know they've been heard. Give your full
   attention, make sure you understand their concern
   or question, and then repeat that back to them. This
   lets them know you've truly listened.

4. *Keep your communication style simple and to the
   point.* Don't overcomplicate your response, and avoid
   "insider" language, such as acronyms or ministry
   names that a person new to the church won't understand. They may easily get confused or overwhelmed
   by their first-time exposure to your church's culture.
   Don't throw them into the deep end of the pool.

5. *Aim to respond within twenty-four hours whenever
   possible.* That's especially tough on weekends. But
   we live in a culture of instant communication,
   and people typically expect a reply within a day of
   making contact. If you'll be unavailable for more
   than a day, provide an alternate contact if you can.
   There's nothing as frustrating as trying to express
   a concern only to be forced to wait for several days
   before you can talk to someone.

6. *Express gratitude for them taking the time to reach
   out and contact you.* Say "thank you" multiple
   times. Remember, they're doing us a favor, because
   we genuinely want to know what our visitors are
   experiencing. If they're encountering obstacles
   or frustrations, we want to take those seriously.
   Express your gratitude and your desire to improve.

7. *Resist appearing defensive when receiving constructive feedback.* There'll be times when the feedback you receive has a critical edge. Try to remain humble and listen, seeking to learn what you can from what's shared. Respond with gentleness and respect, but don't take every critical comment or suggestion personally. Consider what's said in light of the whole, and seek to learn from it.

Since much of our communication today is done by email, below are some examples of emails that illustrate how we respond to concerns and questions people raise.

Email #1: Keri emailed to share her appreciation for Andy and to express some challenges she's facing in her life. We responded with encouragement and by offering to serve her by mailing her a book Andy had written.

Hi Keri,

I'm so glad you wrote! Thank you for your kind words. The *Brand:new* message ("What does love require of me?") was actually one of my personal favorites as well.

Thanks also for sharing about the challenges you've faced. That's a lot for any one human to handle! Despite what you've been through, it's awesome to hear about the breakthroughs you've experienced. My hope is that you'll continue down the road of self-discovery and that you'll stay free from the things that have kept you down in the past.

If you're open to it, I'd love to send you a book that

Andy wrote. I think it could add some value based on what you've shared. If so, what's your mailing address?

Thanks again for reaching out, Keri. Enjoy the rest of your week!

Email #2: Joan emailed to share personal details about recent choices she'd made in response to hearing a talk by Andy. We offered her some online resources to help her continue to make good decisions for her life.

Hi Joan,

Thank you so much for your recent email.

It's exciting to hear how you've chosen to take responsibility for your decisions, which is not always easy. Have you had the chance to check out our message archives on our website? Based on what you've shared, I've listed a few series you may be interested in, starting with:

- *Starting Over*
- *Ask It*
- *Your Move*
- *Taking Responsibility for Your Life*

I hope these suggestions will be helpful. Please don't hesitate to reach out if there's anything else I can do for you. We're rooting for you, Joan!

People feel led to contact churches with all kinds of concerns. The needs and questions can seem endless. But in every situation, the responses we give should always maintain the same high standard of directness, timeliness, and personal concern.

YOUR TURN

1. Think again about each of the personas you created in session two. For each of them, think of a particular concern or question the person might have after visiting your church. As a group, write the contents of the two email messages these personas might write:

Primary:

Secondary:

2. Next, take a few moments to write an email response to each of those messages. Remember to be direct and personal in how you word your message.

Primary:

Secondary:

3. Finally, as a group, compare your email responses. What can you learn from one another's responses?

Conclusion

W hat does your church obsess over?

What is your church preoccupied with?

Churches for churched people obsess over the most frivolous, inconsequential things. It's why you dread your board meetings, your elder meetings, and your committee meetings. You rarely talk about anything important. You're managing *found* people. I know you care about *unfound* people in your heart, but do you care about them in your schedule, your programming, your preaching style, or your budget? Do you know how much difference the care you feel in your heart makes in the life of someone far from God? None at all.

Do you really want to spend the rest of your ministry years feeling something you don't do anything about? Do you really want to spend your life managing what *was* lost to the neglect of what's *still* lost?

If I could make a wish for your church that I knew would come true, I would wish that the loudest, rowdiest, most emotionally charged celebrations in your gatherings would be in response to people going public with their faith through baptism. I want you to be able to turn to your spouse or to someone on your team who's shared the journey with you and say, "What if?" What if we had refused to act boldly? What if we had refused to change? What if we hadn't allowed God to break our hearts?

Look what we would have missed.

Look what they might have missed!

When we began in session one, I asked you to consider a question: What's the faith of a generation worth? So I'll put the challenge before you right now.

- Are you really content to spend the rest of your life doing church the way you've always done it?
- Do you want to continue designing services and programming that appeal only to churched people?
- Do you want to spend another season of ministry doing things that make unbelievers unnecessarily uncomfortable because it's comfortable for you?

Or

- Are you ready to try new things and possibly fail at a few?
- Is there part of you that desires to step away from the familiar and predictable to embrace something new?
- Do you want to be part of a team that creates a church unchurched people love to attend?

My hope is that our time together has awakened, or reawakened, something in you that's willing to take on something *hard*, *expensive*, and *messy*. Something you can't manage.

Something that forces you to pray as you've never prayed before.

To implement some of these changes will require a bold vision. You'll need to make changes. You'll wrestle with tough questions. But as you learn to "assume they're in the room," you'll begin to evaluate everything through the eyes and ears of the unchurched. Things will get a bit crazy. And you'll love it. And you'll never again be content with anything less than being a church unchurched people love to attend—an irresistible church.

& YOUR TURN

1. As your team has journeyed together through *Going Deep and Wide*, what has been the most valuable takeaway for you?

2. How would you summarize your personal vision and commitment for making your church a place where unchurched people feel welcome and where they love to be?

3. What can your group agree on as the most important action steps to take in response to what you've learned from *Going Deep and Wide*? What assignments, priorities, and time frames do you need to establish?

Appendix A:

GOING DEEP RESOURCES

I f you are interested in resources that will help those in your church go deep and grow in their faith, here are three resources to consider.

FIVE THINGS GOD USES TO GROW YOUR FAITH

Five Things God Uses to Grow Your Faith is a small group video-based Bible study (DVD and participant's guide/six sessions) that establishes the biblical case for five things God uses to grow an unshakable faith in you. Imagine how different your outlook on life would be if you had absolute confidence that God was with you. Imagine how differently you would respond to difficulties, temptations, and even good things if you knew with certainty that God was in all of it and

was planning to leverage it for good. In other words, imagine what it would be like to have *perfect* faith.

This study will help those who want to grow more deeply in their understanding of how God works through pivotal circumstances in our lives, through our personal relationships with one another, through practical teaching, through private disciplines, and through personal ministry we offer to others.

CHRISTIAN

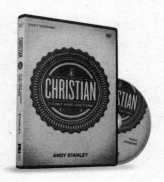

Christian is a small group video-based Bible study (DVD and participant's guide/eight sessions) that examines the characteristics Jesus used to define those who follow him and the implications for believers today. In *Christian*, you'll learn the following:

- What one word should be descriptive of every Christian
- How Jesus' followers should treat those who are outside the faith
- Why people love Jesus but can't stand his followers

What does it mean to be Christian? Curiously, the term is never used in Scripture. Instead, Christian was a label used by outsiders to define Jesus' followers. Jesus referenced *disciple* as the key word he used to describe his supporters along with the fact that they would be known for their love—a novel concept for their time—and ours today.

This study unpacks the qualities Jesus prescribes for his followers that make them unique. And it challenges you to ask: what if believers today embodied these traits?

How to Be Rich

How to Be Rich is a church campaign featuring a four-session video (enhanced by three full-length sermons by Andy Stanley) as well as a book that includes a four-session small group discussion guide.

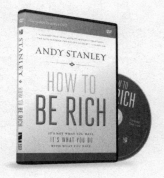

Most of us are richer than we realize. But we might think: *rich is the other guy.* Rich is having more than we currently have. If that's the case, we can be rich and not know or feel it. We can be rich and not act like it. And that's a problem. Andy encourages us to not just *be* rich, but he helps us learn to be *good* at it. As the apostle Paul wrote, "Command them to do good, to be rich in good deeds, and to be generous and willing to share" (1 Timothy 6:18).

Appendix B

THE AGILE APOLOGETIC: AN INTERVIEW WITH ANDY STANLEY*

Interview by Paul J. Pastor

A ndy Stanley crafted a six-part message series aimed directly at the growing number of religiously unaffiliated—the so-called "nones"—titled *Who Needs God* (WhoNeedsGod. com). The series has drawn wide attention and discussion, both for facing tough topics, including the "new atheism," head on, and for Stanley's controversial opinion that appealing strictly to the authority of the Bible when preaching to outsiders is a losing strategy.

Outreach contributing writer Paul J. Pastor spoke with Stanley to talk through the changing pastoral needs of younger generations and why today's leaders need to rediscover an agile apologetic.

---

* Reprinted from *Outreach* magazine, February 5, 2017. Used with permission.

Who Needs God is a gutsy title for a megachurch message series. What was the vision for it?

This teaching series was designed for people who weren't in our building. It is for the "nones," the 25 to 30 percent of our population who may have grown up in church but have decided they're not interested. They're not atheists or agnostics, just unaffiliated. We decided to do a series of messages for them. While most of the people in our church aren't in that group, *everyone* knows people who are—their family, friends, coworkers, neighbors.

For context, every week we have about 24,000 adults at church in person on our Atlanta area campuses, plus about 20,000 who watch online. Then, because of television (we follow *Saturday Night Live* [SNL], so when they have a big week, we do too), we can swing from 600,000 to 1 million people just in the post-SNL audience. Because of that, we're thinking of all those dynamics when we create our Sunday morning environments.

It was different for us to talk to an audience who was not primarily in the building. It created a bit of understandable confusion, especially for anyone who dropped in to the middle of the series.

"Who needs God?" is a key question the nones are asking. Answering it has also been a distinctive of our ministry from the beginning, since we've always believed it was our mission to keep the lowest possible rungs on the ladder as people begin to explore spirituality. That has nothing to do with dumbing down sermons, picking or choosing doctrines, or avoiding the whole counsel of God, as we're sometimes accused of doing, but it has everything to do with our approach.

Today, the numbers show that there is decreasing interest in Christianity. But there is extraordinary interest in spirituality. We're playing in that space—leaving breadcrumbs for people to follow back into authentic faith in Christ. In a very real sense, we're hosting others in our space and making room for them. We have to assume that they have been exposed to deep criticisms and attacks on the Bible and Christianity.

Was there a particular moment when you realized you needed to address challenges to faith in order to engage those outside the church?

About eight years ago, I watched a video of new-atheist Sam Harris lecturing in a university. About half of his lecture was about Christianity, and about half of that half was about Scripture. I watched him, it seemed, dismantle the Bible. He's so smart, so articulate, so quick on his feet. *Even the above-average Christian*, I thought, *couldn't sit through this without their faith being practically destroyed.*

His critique came across as devastating, but it also contained all kinds of distortions and inaccuracies. But they were points we simply don't cover in church. I thought about our own student ministry, and knew that I wasn't preparing our high school kids to sit through a lecture like that in college and walk out with their faith intact. I was convicted.

That was a defining moment. In response, I began to change my approach, stepping back from leveraging the authority of Scripture in favor of talking about the history and the people behind the story of Scripture, particularly the event of Christ's resurrection. It's not about abandoning Scripture, it's laying a foundation that's defensible in our culture, where you may have only five minutes—at best—to defend what you believe.

That's helpful. Unpack the deconversion process a bit more.

People don't simply leave faith; they leave a *version* of faith. We all know that there are multiple versions of the Christian faith. When you hear a deconversion story—someone who went off to school, or met somebody, or read a book, or moved away, or whatever—they are nearly always walking away from a version of Christianity. Consequently, they have a skewed version or vision of God that they are leaving.

I started listening to the *Life After God* podcast a while back, a show for atheists and agnostics, and have recently been texting back and forth with Ryan Bell. At the time this article goes live, I'll have been a guest on the podcast. One section, called the "Ex-Files," focuses on deconversion stories. As a pastor, it's so clear listening to it that these stories of deconversion are people leaving versions of Christianity that most Christians would completely be against, as well. When I hear some of these stories, I think, *Heck. I would have left that too!*

We all think our version of Christianity is the right one. But we can't all be correct. So to address people who have left the faith or are considering doing so, it's important to understand *what* specifically about the faith they're leaving. *Who Needs God* focuses on this. My big point at the front end of the series is to point out that it's possible that a person has left faith for the wrong reason.

Often, I might say to a person that what they left *needed* to be left, because it wasn't really Christianity to begin with.

I want to help people differentiate between what is worth leaving the faith over, and what are not fundamentals or essentials of faith. When the nonessentials get equated with the essentials, we give people excuses to leave unnecessarily. I'd like to ferret out those distinctions up front.

Talk about balancing the needs of those seeking and those who believe in relation to apologetics.

Great question. That's one of the reasons behind the title of my book *Deep and Wide*. We often assume that people either have a verse-by-verse "deep" church or a "wide" giant megachurch. But when we read the Gospels, we see that Jesus is both deep and wide in his ministry. Crowds were a constant feature of his ministry. So I don't think of this in terms of a balance. We are out to create churches that unchurched people love to attend, but we're not a church for unchurched people.

Paul, who planted so many churches, taught us that "one another" is at the center of church life. The activity of the church is centered on community—forgive, accept, care for, encourage, bear with, restore, carry one another's burdens. Everybody I've ever met wants to be in that kind of community.

Imagine a world where people were skeptical of what we believed, but envious of how well we treated one another, and *shocked* at how well we treated them! That's what the church is about. We can maintain our identity while looking for opportunities to include everyone in our sense of community. But we need to understand how to host outsiders well in our environments.

Let's focus on that idea of "hosting" for a moment. As our culture dechurches, will we be hosting those outside of Christianity more? If so, how do we grow in our skills to host?

Absolutely! We will be hosting more, in many different contexts. Pastors, if you want outsiders to be in your audience, they need to know that *you* know that they're there.

Welcoming non-Christians has been a distinctive of our ministry for many years. I've talked about the progression of "foyer ? living room ? kitchen" for some time. Think of hosting in your church like you host in your house: Guests come into the foyer, which is designed to welcome. Then, into the living room, which is for more formal conversation and socializing. But the kitchen? That is where life *really* happens.

When you host people in your home, you don't abandon your values or what you believe, but you also don't ignore them. You don't make them do all the work of finding their way around your house. You spend extra energy on them. You don't abandon them. I think every church has to embrace hosting others to some extent—the question is, "*Who* are you hosting?" Today's reality is that we are hosting unbelievers, skeptics and post-Christian people all the time. We can't change our beliefs or convictions, but we can certainly work to host them well in our environments.

What's the first step to doing that well?

Examine our assumptions. We all know that assumptions are tricky things. They inform our decisions, but we often don't realize how, because we don't take the time to think through them. Church leaders need to give up three assumptions when it comes to preaching to or engaging with the dechurched.

First, we still preach like we assume that people view Scripture as authoritative. They do not. Now, whenever I say that, I get in trouble. People hear me saying that Scripture isn't authoritative. I'm not saying that!

I'm simply acknowledging a fact: Many people still respect the Bible but no longer consider it authoritative. Assuming it's an authority for their life will be a nonstarter. But once we dispense with that assumption, we can step back to see that there are plenty of places to get traction in minds and hearts. In the old days, people really only heard about the Bible in church. But now, because we have so much access to information, it's foolish to assume that a preacher's statements about the Bible are going to be the only thing shaping someone's understanding of it.

For example, Bart Erhman, the agnostic biblical scholar, has become a familiar cultural face—he's been on late-night TV with Stephen Colbert—primetime, millennial viewing—to talk about his book *Jesus Before the Gospels.* Here's a conversation about the Bible and Jesus, and of course his whole pitch is that the Gospels can't be trusted as historical documents. In the old days there were never those kinds of questions in the broader culture.

We also have to quit assuming that "they" are "out there." "Assume they're in the room" has become my mantra. I was at a funeral recently at a large church. As we drove out, there were signs that said, "You are now entering the mission field." That's completely false, and has been for a long time—because "they" are present at and watching our church gatherings constantly. They are in your church, with you, with their questions, their doubts, their conflicts between the Bible and science, all of it. They are visiting, curious, listening to your podcast, checking you out online. Assuming that we're the team "in here" getting ready to go "out there" and do ministry isn't in touch with today's reality. Assume they are in the room.

The third assumption is that a person has to believe before they follow. Nothing could be clearer in the New Testament, particularly in the Gospels. Jesus invited people to follow before they believed. In our messaging, are we inviting people who are outsiders to follow?

Everybody can take a step to follow Jesus. I'm not offended when I have people tell me that I'm a great motivational speaker and that they just "filter out the Jesus stuff." I can't make people fall in love with Jesus, but if they keep coming, I'll keep setting up the dates. We'll keep the rungs low on the ladder and encourage them to take the baby steps of following him. *Follow* precedes *believe.*

Let's return to the point you've recently taken flak on—how we use the Bible in our preaching. What is the faithful path forward for preachers who are speaking to listeners who doubt the Bible's authority?

Not to change what we believe, but how we communicate. Once upon a time, there was a version of our faith that was rooted in an event, not the record of the event. The record of the resurrection followed the event of the resurrection by years. Christianity grew like crazy before the Bible, as we know it, existed. Historically, what launched our movement was an event. I'm *in no way* discounting the Bible by saying that.

In the old days, when pretty much everyone in culture

respected the Bible and saw it as authoritative, this discussion wasn't that important. But in the Information Age, when we can't count on scriptural authority being accepted by our culture, we need to return to what we did during the first, second and third centuries—an apologetic that pointed back to the event. Think of Paul in 1 Corinthians 15. He says that if there is no resurrection of the dead, then Christ is not risen, and our preaching—which means our religion, our faith, this whole thing—is in vain. It's all pointless without the event of the resurrection.

The resurrection as a real event is everything. It's where we get traction today. I believe it's the most defensible event associated with Christianity. And coincidentally, it's the most *important* event. I think we need to stop fighting about so many other things and simply stand upon the resurrection. Why? Because in that event, our faith stands.

When I talk about this with non-Christians or people reconsidering faith, this makes sense to them. When I talk about it with educated Christians, for some reason it makes many of them nervous. While I own my own ambiguity on this point in the past, and don't claim to be great at talking about it, I'm still so convinced that this is a vital point for us to recover for our outreach.

Once you have traction, it's not necessarily that complicated to move forward. I highlight that following Jesus has made my life better and has made me better at life. I'm convinced that's true for anyone. That's the introduction—come and follow. Forgive, and your life will be better because of it. Let go of bitterness and submit to others—your life will be better. We can go on and on.

Imagine if everyone in the U.S. decided to put others ahead of themselves. Our culture would change. Following Jesus makes lives, nations, the world better. That in itself can't convince someone that Jesus is the Son of God, but it does get their attention. Where to go from there? Back to our belief in the power and historical reality of the resurrection. "Come and follow."

What are you hearing from new believers as to why they are becoming Christians?

Those reasons never change, although trends may shift a bit. One of the things we do when we baptize new believers is show a video of each of them to the church detailing their story of faith. It's a requirement—we won't baptize you unless you're willing to make that public statement in that way. Honestly, it keeps our numbers low, but it makes our baptism impact very high. It becomes an extraordinary celebration. We baptize one to three people per service at all of our campuses every other Sunday. We put baptisteries in our middle school and high school environments so younger believers are telling their stories to their peers as they are getting baptized. We take baptism as a public declaration *super* seriously, and we want them to go public in front of their public.

Based on thousands of those baptism videos—and I'm thinking of college students and older here—there are the old, consistent stories. Pain. Brokenness. The dead ends of skepticism. Recovering from bad church experiences. Dealing with loss. Divorce. Business fallout. Losing children. I hear all the typical stories of the Prodigal Son, who had everything he ever wanted until suddenly he woke up and realized that he was missing what he needed most: a connection to his Father.

The church that has the low rungs on the ladder and is the most welcoming, that has the best reputation in the community, those are the ones that will be doing the most evangelism. Brokenness leads to repentance. Sorrow causes everybody to look up. That's an on-ramp to faith. We need to capitalize on that in terms of how we talk about things, how we respond to people. One of our pastors here said years ago that we need to "walk toward the messes" in people's lives. That's right on. That's what Jesus did.

One of the digs that people make about megachurches like ours is that we "don't make it about the people." That is so not true, and it's an insult to everybody who attends a megachurch. It's like saying they're all just sheep, who'll do anything the guy on the stage says. When I read those kinds of things, I want to invite people to our elders' meetings, our stewardship meetings. These are doctors, lawyers, CEOs. People who are new Christians or have been Christians forever. These are not stupid people. These are not the kind of people to do whatever the guy with the microphone is saying. We care so much about our community. We see opportunities everywhere for connection.

How do leaders prepare (or re-prepare) for ministry in our changing culture?

They need to examine the barriers—often through assumptions like I mentioned earlier—that stand in the way of people coming or returning to faith.

What I want to know as a lead pastor is what makes it

difficult or easy for you to invite your unchurched friends—
regardless of race, belief or background—to our church.
James said in Acts 15:19, a verse that hangs in all our build-
ings: "It is my judgment, therefore, that we should not make
it difficult for the Gentiles who are turning to God" (NIV).

Think about this, from James the brother of Jesus to the
apostles: "We should not make it difficult . . ." This is in relation to the Gentiles—who to those early Jewish Christians
were the foreigner, the immigrant, the ones of different color
and religion. That context is so timely for us today. We can
see them as the "demographic challenge." That means that
we should take down all the barriers we can.

That's the life verse for our churches. We're not removing
the barrier of the gospel—that's offensive in itself—but we are
working to keep the offense *limited* to the gospel, not how
the parking lot works, not how we check kids in, not the fact
that everybody on the stage is white and so on. What can
we do to reduce the barriers? A church staff can't fully know
that. But the people can. We need to know how to survey
them and get core people in a room from time to time and
ask the questions that no leader wants to hear the answer
to, because we'd like to think that we're doing everything
perfectly already.

Let's make sure that we aren't making it difficult for
those who are turning to God.

How do apologetics relate to not making it difficult to believe?

We pastors (I think it's the way we're trained) have a knack
for devaluing what unchurched people value. That's a *terrible*

mistake. It makes me cringe. We should never devalue or make fun of people's life assumptions. It's like raising kids. You can correct your kids constantly and be right every time. And if you do the right thing the wrong way, your kid won't come home as soon as they're old enough to get out of the house. You will have made your point. And lost your influence.

You increase your influence by valuing what people value, and slowly, over time, helping them see that there's another way to think. You can do that without being critical. Look at Jesus. The only times he was overtly critical was with religious leaders, when he was confronting their hypocrisy and theology. But the tax gatherers and sinners? He started where they were. With stories, with meals, with spending time in their homes and allowing them to join his friends. That resulted in their emotional connection with Jesus, which is so instructive for us.

Can you give a practical example of that principle? How would it look in a message?

When I talk about sex, dating or other relationship stuff, it often makes sense to talk about the issue of believers marrying a nonbeliever. The traditional approach to that in a preaching setting is to say to the believers listening something like, "Ladies, if you're a Christian, you shouldn't date a non-Christian guy. Gentlemen, the same principle applies to non-Christian women." Well, if you assume that nonbelievers are in the room, you've just offended all of them, whether you've meant it or not, because what they just heard is, "We're better than you."

The better way is to consider that my authority isn't with the unchurched people in the room, it's with Christians.

So, what do I say instead? "Hey, if you're here today and you're not really a religious person, I advise you not to date a Christian. Here's why. Christians are going to do a bait and switch on you. They're going to try to change you. If you marry a Christian, they're going to want you to raise your kids in church, and . . ."

You see where I'm going. My point is that there is a way to talk about anything with the unchurched people in the room in mind, that is apologetic in nature, as long as we're careful about unearthing assumptions that at times cause us to talk about "them" and "they" in terms that would be unnecessarily offensive. A simple rephrase can get your point across without devaluing them.

Another example—justice. Everyone, believer or not, longs for justice to be done. So what if we turned to the unbelievers in the room and said—"Hey, whether you believe or not, you should *want* Christianity to be true! Why? Because if what Jesus said about the end is true, perfect justice *wins.*" It's a different angle, but a productive one.

Let's go deeper on the justice point, which is the theme of one of your messages in *Who Needs God*. How do we address justice honestly, when Christianity's history is seen as (and is) tarnished on that point?

Sam Harris' book *Letters to a Christian Nation* is a little 90-page book. Pastors should read it for two reasons. First, if you can keep your own faith after reading it, good for you *[laughs]*, but second, if you want to have some assumptions dispelled as you relate to a post-Christian culture, this book will help, especially on any of our assumptions related to the authority of Scripture in nonbelievers' lives. He goes for the jugular regarding the assumptions Christians make in a world where, he argues, our faith has created pain and suffering.

The simple answer (but it's not very satisfying) is that the truth that empties into the bucket is different than the bucket. We're the bucket. The truth is truth. We are not perfect buckets. Christians have the best answer in the world for why there is pain and suffering and evil.

But with that said, there is no justification for our own injustices of history. We must own that, especially since so many current voices are so quick to point out our faith's historical failings. But back to the apologetic question—which worldview does not have the same kind of stuff in their history? None that I know of. Welcome to the real world.

Our promise is that someday God will make all right. That's the promise of Christianity as punctuated by a resurrected Savior.

You encourage those outside the faith that "you belong at church before you believe." Tell us more.

This goes back to Jesus' invitation to follow. When I say that with Christian leaders or folks looking for "gotcha" moments, they immediately spin into, "Oh, but what is the church? A fellowship of believers. And now you're saying that people belong to the church without being Christians," and so on.

No. That's jumping way ahead. I'm not talking about joining the church necessarily. I'm not talking about everybody playing every role in the local church. This is a front-line message to people who have shown up nervous, and are wondering if these people are their people or not. *Will they like me? Can I bring my kids? Can I try a small group?* There are multiple circles in every church for a person to belong before they believe. So let's state that clearly.

It's our conviction to even let nonbelievers serve in many capacities. One of my favorite stories out of the *Who Needs God* series was of a woman who wrote me a letter after her second week there. She's an atheist in the medical profession. She told me about how she responded to the content. I met with her, and a couple months later she signed up to go on a medical missions trip with our church. She's still an atheist. But she's going to go with our group to China, to an orphanage outside of Beijing to give the nationals working there a break because they're there 24/7 with disabled kids. Get this—she's going to spend 10 days with a group of wonderful Christians serving in an orphanage. She already feels like she belongs. Even though she does not yet believe.

There are concentric circles of inclusion and involvement. We've worked hard to find excuses to say "yes" to getting people engaged and involved, and in the community. "Where two or more are gathered, there I am in the midst of them," Jesus said, and I think we see that in our worship and gatherings. When people see the "one anothers" being lived out, the obstacles come down, amazing things happen and they meet Jesus.

Are you hopeful for the future of the church in our culture?

Absolutely. The challenges are real, but we don't have to freak out at the demographic research or any other points that might discourage. We do have to change our approach to ministry, though. There are huge signs of hope across the globe for Christianity, but even here where the nones are on the rise, there is hope. People get methodology and theology confused all the time, and then get upset when you start changing methodology. They're two different things. Theology should inform ministry, but if it limits whom you minister to, then you have the wrong theology. Just ask Jesus.

The good news is that there are other approaches that will create traction and reduce tension with culture, but our current evangelical approach is becoming less relevant because it makes too many assumptions that we don't even need to make. The only thing that is discouraging to me is not what's happening in the broader culture, but seeing so many Christian leaders who are so dug in to a version of faith, methodology and apologetics that they feel that they're losing something essential. Consequently, they're going to lose influence.

There are so many cool things happening with church planting, so many young entrepreneurial leaders who are wanting to make a difference and give up what is nonessential to make an impact on their community. The next 10 to 15 years are going to be exciting. But a lot will change. A lot must change. But there is so much hope for the future of our faith.

Honestly? I'm so excited about it. I wish I were 35 again.

Notes

1. "The Unaffiliated," *2014 Religious Landscape Study*, May 12, 2015.
2. Alister E. McGrath, *Mere Apologetics: How to Help Seekers and Skeptics Find Faith* (Grand Rapids: Baker, 2012), 32.
3. John O'Sullivan, "Christianity, Post-Christianity, and the Future of the West," *National Review*, www .nationalreview.com/article/366263/our-post-christian -society-john-osullivan.
4. "State of the Church 2016," *Barna Group*, www.barna .com/research/state-church-2016/.
5. *The Bible in America: The Changing Landscape of Bible Perceptions and Engagement* (Barna Group, 2016).
6. *The Bible in America*, 8.
7. *The Bible in America*, 56–58.
8. *The Bible in America*, 89.
9. See Rodney Stark, *The Rise of Christianity* (San Francisco: HarperSanFrancisco, 1997).

Deep & Wide

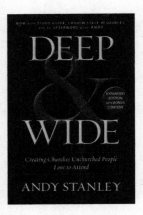

Andy Stanley's bestselling and award-winning vision for the local church is now available in softcover. New bonus content includes a study guide, church staff helps, and an interview with Andy on the most frequently asked questions about *Deep and Wide*.

With surprising candor and transparency pastor Andy Stanley explains how one of America's largest churches began with a high-profile divorce and a church split.

But that's just the beginning...

Deep and Wide provides church leaders with an in-depth look into North Point Community Church and its strategy for creating churches unchurched people absolutely love to attend.

Available in stores and online!

Irresistible Faith

Irresistible Faith takes readers on a fascinating journey back in time to understand what once made faith in Jesus irresistible, how the early church turned the world upside-down, and how we can recover that same faith today.

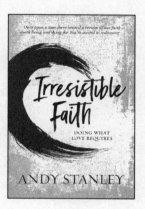